Make effective
decisions

Make effective decisions

decisions

How to weigh up the options and make the right choice

A & C Black • London

© A & C Black Publishers Ltd 2007

First published in 2007 by
A & C Black Publishers Ltd
38 Soho Square
London W1D 3HB

A CIP record for this book is available from the British Library.

ISBN-10: 0–7136–8148–9
ISBN-13: 978–0–7136–8148–2

Design by Fiona Pike, Pike Design, Winchester
Typeset by RefineCatch Limited, Bungay, Suffolk
Printed in Italy by Rotolito

This book is produced using paper that is made from wood grown in managed, sustainable forests. It is natural, renewable and recyclable. The logging and manufacturing processes conform to the environmental regulations of the country of origin.

Contents

What sort of decision-maker are you?   vi

1 Getting to the heart of an issue   1

2 Looking at a problem from different perspectives   10

3 Asking the right questions   18

4 Using proven problem-solving techniques   28

5 Making good decisions under pressure   39

6 Conducting a cost/benefit analysis   48

7 Avoiding procrastination   58

8 Getting your message across   68

Where to find more help   79

Index   83

What sort of decision-maker are you?

Answer the questions and work out where you come on the scale, then read the guidance points.

How far do you trust your gut instinct?
a) Not at all.
b) To a certain extent.
c) Implicitly.

What's your approach to a complicated issue?
a) I ignore it and hope it goes away.
b) I try to look at it systematically and rationally.
c) I follow my intuition.

What decision-making methods do you use?
a) Familiar, tried and tested techniques.
b) A variety of methods.
c) Methods schmethods!

What do you look for when solving a problem?
a) The path of least resistance.
b) A solution that takes into account the long term, too.
c) Whatever will resolve my immediate problem.

How do you react to pressure?
a) Not well—if it all goes wrong it's my fault!
b) I'm usually able to keep things in perspective.
c) I enjoy the adrenaline rush.

Do you canvass others' opinions when decision making?
a) Of course! I ask as many people as possible.
b) Yes. They are important to me.
c) I'm confident enough not to need to ask others.

How often do you find yourself putting off making a decision?
a) Twice a week.
b) Twice a month.
c) Never.

a = 1, b = 2, c = 3

Now add up your scores.

- **7–11**: You take decision making very seriously—but it clearly makes you nervous. Perhaps a more assertive approach, while still keeping your ability to take on board what others have to say, would make your life easier. To increase your confidence, build your arsenal of techniques by reading chapters **1** and **4**. The advice in chapter **5** will help you keep calm under pressure, while chapter **7** has tips for tackling procrastination. And remember that you *are* allowed to settle for a compromise, and even to make mistakes once in a while!

- **12–16**: Well done—you seem to be fairly comfortable at making decisions. Chapter **2** will help you to ensure that you look at the problem from many different angles. Take your skills further by learning more about analysing the costs and benefits of a proposal before coming to a decision (chapter **6**).

- **17–21**: Your confidence is great—but make sure you don't overdo it. Don't think you know it all: read about the variety of different decision-making techniques in chapters **1** and **4**. It's crucial to look at the whole picture: examine your assumptions, think long term, and look at the effects your decisions have on others. Chapters **2** and **3** will help you to look at the situation from different angles.

Getting to the heart of an issue

Being able to make good decisions is an essential workplace skill. Whatever your role, there will be times when you need to get to grips with an issue and decide on the best course of action. If you need to make a decision, your first step should be to analyse the situation. These first three chapters will help you to do just that, while the following chapters look in more detail at decision-making techniques.

In organisations there are often set procedures for making decisions, which minimise the amount of time spent on original thinking. However, constant 'quick fixes' are not a recipe for increased profitability and organisational growth.

'Fire fighting' in the workplace creates an illusion of industry: lots of busy people carrying out lots of tasks. The energy of such an environment can seduce us into thinking that nothing further can be done to increase productivity other than to work harder and faster. But this isn't the case: wherever you work, you can improve your efficiency by taking time to think through situations from first principles and making

**decisions that have lasting positive effects.
Read on to find out how.**

Step one: Question the status quo

Understanding the root cause of an issue and coming to a decision based on that knowledge will more than repay the time and effort spent in identifying it. In some businesses, things have been done the same way for years and years, and the reasons for doing something a particular way have become lost in the annals of time. Even if the context has changed, the same methods are adopted without question, even though they don't make sense any more. The existence of these habits is often exposed by comments such as: 'But that's the way we've always done it!' By flagging up how ineffectual these habits are and highlighting the amount of time they waste, you're likely to be able to persuade people to do things differently.

Think of the way a computer keyboard is laid out. We still use the QWERTY configuration, although most people do not touch-type. Two-finger typing is not assisted by a layout that is based on the frequency of letter usage. Indeed, the fact that physical keys are used at all is an unnecessary feature of the keyboard. These are two examples of habits that are rooted in history and have not been re-evaluated in the light of modern technology.

Ask a few questions of the situation. For instance:

- Is something happening that constantly distracts attention from the 'real' job?
- Are you trying to outwit processes or procedures?
- Are you spending more time fire fighting than producing results?
- Do you have to wait until the end of the day before you can start being productive?
- Are simple activities taking too long to perform?
- Would removing a root cause cost less than dealing with the symptom?

Step two: Analyse the root cause(s)

Root cause analysis may help you to answer the questions above and get to the heart of the issue in question. It encourages you to look beneath the surface and understand what's causing it to appear. Systems thinking like this does not look at the elements of a problem in isolation; rather, it looks at the *dynamics* of the issue and the *relationships* between the causes and effects.

Root cause analysis is a logical deductive technique which helps you to identify what, how, and why something happens. It helps to reveal that part of a problem which, once resolved, will prevent it from recurring.

There are four stages to root cause analysis:

1 Collecting data. To do a worthwhile analysis, you will need to gain a thorough understanding of the situation.

2 **Charting the causes.** Chart the events and processes which lead to the situation. Use a flowchart so you can clearly see the sequences of events.

3 **Identifying the root cause.** Examine the flowchart. If you have analysed and distilled the data correctly, you should be able to see the root of the problem or issue.

4 **Generating and implementing recommendations.** Although you may not be responsible for the implementation, unless you follow up by making sure that action is taken, your decision-making efforts will have been in vain.

A good root cause analysis also considers human issues, such as people's abilities and motivations. Human bottlenecks can be caused by limited abilities, inadequate training, a lack of interest, or an absence of recognition and reward. An elegant solution is useless unless it is carried out effectively by people; it's therefore crucial to factor in the human side of the issue.

TOP TIP
When we are under pressure, we often take a 'sticking plaster' approach to solving a problem. However, this does nothing to resolve the matter in the longer term. A problem will recur over and over again until we understand and resolve its cause.

Step three: Use a cause and effect diagram

There are many different styles of cause and effect diagram, but the basic aim of each is to help you to look at a situation from a wider perspective and identify the features that underpin it. You may have a preferred style of your own which will help you to 'see' the problem.

One type of cause and effect diagram is Edward de Bono's **concept fan**. To create a concept fan, draw a circle on the left of the page and write the problem inside it. Then draw lines radiating from the circle towards the right of the page, leading to different potential solutions (see chapters 3 and 4 for tips on generating ideas). You can then assess each of the solutions in relation to the context. Creating the fan means that patterns can be seen more clearly, often revealing a more effective, long-term solution.

To help you to trace the causes and chart the effects, ask the following questions:

- Why did this situation occur?
- What is the history behind the situation?
- What happened immediately *before* the situation occurred?
- What other people or issues are affected?
- What would change the nature of the situation?

- Is there any significance in the timing of the situation?
- What is the impact of this situation?
- What happened after the situation occurred?
- What would enable the situation to continue to exist?
- What would stop the situation from existing?

Step four: Try the Six Sigma approach

Six Sigma is a disciplined approach to measuring an organisation's performance. Part of the approach uses a technique called the '5 Whys'. This allows you to get to the root of an issue very quickly. It was made popular in the 1970s by the Toyota Production System, where it was used to diagnose the cause of a problem by asking (as you may have guessed) 'Why?' five times over. Children have also perfected this technique!

The reason that 'Why?' is asked successively is that very often the answer to the first 'Why?' leads on to another 'Why?' The more it's asked, the greater the distillation and the closer you get to the heart of the issue. This simple technique is very easy to learn, and quick to apply. To use it, start with the effect and work back towards the cause as shown below:

The situation: A company's ordering process involves many people.

The problem: It is time-consuming, and also subject to human error and delay.

■ **Why** *do we use paper requisition slips to request resources?*

Because we need a record of what has been requested.

■ **Why** *do we need a record of what has been requested?*

So that we can monitor the use of resources.

■ **Why** *do we need to do this?*

So that we can monitor the cost and plan their purchase.

■ **Why** *do we need to do this?*

So that we can get the best deal from the supplier.

■ **Why** *can't we do this electronically?*

Why indeed . . .!

Common mistakes

✗ **You don't invest enough time in looking at a problem**

Short-term pressures can make you think that you don't have time to identify the source of a problem. It's also very easy to make a knee-jerk decision if you're under a lot of pressure. If you can, take just a little bit more time to think about the issue systematically. This will mean that you can resolve it in the longer term and release yourself from the tyranny of constant fire fighting.

✗ You solve the wrong problem

Not thinking about the cause of a problem in enough detail can result in a false start when you are trying to solve it. Do a 'reality check' with an experienced colleague or your boss to ensure that you haven't missed anything obvious. This objective view will ensure that you don't spend time solving the wrong problem and have to start all over again!

✗ You open a 'can of worms'

Sometimes the resolution to the problem starts getting out of hand. It is important to put boundaries around the time you spend solving a problem and the level of your intervention so that it doesn't start to take over your working day. Keep in mind the cost/benefit equation (see chapter 6 for more on this). If it starts costing too much in terms of time, resources, and effort, be prepared to settle for a partial solution.

STEPS TO SUCCESS

✔ Think long-term. Partially solving a problem means that it's likely to come back to haunt you.

✔ Take your time to work things through from every angle.

✔ If you're constantly fire fighting at work, it's time to reassess your methods and processes.

✔ Don't get so caught up in searching for the cause of an issue that you neglect your other work. Beware of paralysis by analysis!

✔ Sorting out an issue before making a decision may require more initial input (of time and, probably, money)—but it will be worth it.

Useful links

Root cause analysis:
www.systems-thinking.org
Determine the root cause—the '5 whys':
www.isixsigma.com

Looking at a problem from different perspectives

As decisions usually have a knock-on effect for other people, it's crucial that decision makers are aware of the wider picture.

By taking time to look at a situation from different angles, we give ourselves the opportunity to reach a creative decision. Finding elegant and inventive solutions will help us move beyond the perpetual demands on our time, reduce the pressure we're under, and increase our productivity. If we don't put the effort in, we're likely to get stuck in a rut and become bored. Re-evaluating a situation and gaining fresh ideas brings new energy to the workplace that can result in a greater sense of contribution and satisfaction—and it may bring to light some important issues that have previously been missed. This chapter looks at the best way to analyse a situation from different perspectives.

Step one: Know the value of different perspectives

The anthropologist Ralph Linton said that 'the last thing a fish would notice would be the water'. We get so used to our own worlds that we don't notice the defining features of them!

By being alert to the possibility that there may be other ways of looking at problems, you will send a signal to your brain to be more vigilant and to look at the situation from a wider perspective. Ask yourself:

- Do I have all the information?
- Have I considered all the circumstances?
- Are there flaws in my approach?
- Is the problem recurring and my solution short term?

All these considerations will lead to a fast appraisal and will focus your efforts more effectively.

TOP TIP
Very often, being familiar with a situation results in our doing the same thing over and over again. Sometimes it's helpful to ask someone fresh to the situation to look at the problem. The innocent and obvious question that leads to a creative solution may be the one that you've missed because your

---

**responses have become ingrained. Ask
someone who has had no prior experience of
the situation to share their immediate
thoughts and ideas with you.**

Step two: Be aware of the tools and techniques

A number of techniques are available to help people
see things from different vantage points. Perhaps the
best-known is Edward de Bono's 'six thinking hats'.
This practical approach helps us to look up, out, and
beyond the assumed confines of a problem.

The 'six thinking hats' can be used in meetings, where each
participant 'wears' a different coloured 'hat'. Each hat
triggers different thinking processes. (It doesn't have to be a
real hat. This is a symbolic term!)

- *White Hat:* this is the 'data hat'. The wearer should focus
  on the available information and determine where the
  gaps are. He or she should also look at the patterns and
  trends inherent in a situation and build a future picture
  from this analysis.
- *Red Hat:* this is the 'intuitive hat'. It's up to the wearer to
  introduce feelings and instincts to the process, both
  while arriving at a decision and in considering how others
  will react to that decision.

- *Black Hat:* this is the 'opposing hat'. The wearer should stimulate a critical examination of the decision and seek out errors in the thinking. This reveals the weak points in a plan and enables the development of contingencies.
- *Yellow Hat:* this is the 'positive hat'. The wearer encourages a more optimistic viewpoint that focuses on the benefits and the possibilities that stem from a decision. This can revive the energy of a meeting.
- *Green Hat:* this is the 'creative hat' which allows for innovative ideas and alternative solutions. The wearer should be non-judgemental, and should encourage out-of-the-box thinking.
- *Blue Hat:* this is the chairperson's hat. He or she directs the meeting and makes sure that the right hats are being worn at the right times. If the process is becoming laboured, the person wearing the Blue Hat will intervene and redirect the thinking.

Another technique for thinking about situations from different perspectives is the 'reframing matrix', devised by Michael Morgan.

A reframing matrix is created by writing a question in the middle of a piece of paper, then drawing boxes around the question. Each box is used to consider the issue from a different perspective. In the '4Ps' approach, for example, this would be from the perspectives of the *Product* itself, the *Planning* implications, the *Potential* of the product and the *People* involved with it (either as producers or as consumers). Alternatively, you could use the boxes to see the problem from the perspective of different professional stakeholders (such as *employees*, *customers*, *suppliers*, and *partners*).

TOP TIP
It's important to set your thinking in
the context of the issue you are trying
to resolve. To work out what is relevant
and what is not, look forward and anticipate
the potential outcome of your actions.
If by taking a different perspective a
longer-term solution can be found,
then it is probably a good one
to implement.

Step three: Encourage diversity

In meetings where different perspectives are needed, it is helpful to have as many people from different cultures, professional backgrounds, and interests as possible. Diversity in teams stimulates new and unusual ways of looking at problems. When people from different backgrounds, talents, and passions come together, it is less likely that time-hardened assumptions will endure. They are bound to rankle or disturb someone's sensitivities, which will prompt a thoughtful reconsideration of the issue. Homogeneous teams very often fall into step with each other without comment or challenge. This results in agreements devoid of creativity and militates against invention or discovery.

As the Nobel Prize winner Albert Szent-Gyorgi noted, 'Discovery consists in seeing what everyone else has seen and thinking what no-one else has thought'.

Common mistakes

✗ You assume that those around you have the same attitudes, values, and beliefs as yourself

It can be quite a shock to realise that not everyone thinks like you. Indeed, if you make this assumption you risk being seen as egocentric. When you're under pressure to make a decision, any assumptions you hold will be exposed—especially if you're part of a team of strong-minded, vocal people, each with a different view on things. Be aware of differences in approach and attitude, and make sure that people either share your views or are happy to be in the 'loyal minority'; either way, you want them to support you in your decision making.

✗ You stereotype people

Stereotyping people eclipses the richness of individuality and can result in poor decisions that don't accommodate everybody's views or needs. We stereotype people so that we don't have to spend time getting to know them properly. Although it may enable us to make rapid decisions, it is essentially lazy. When you're taking a decision, therefore, check that your assumptions are shared (or at least understood) by your colleagues so that you are not at risk of making an embarrassing gaffe!

We may think we know someone because we hold a perception based on an observation we have made or an experience we have shared with them in the past. However, we don't know their perspective on the situation under discussion; without this, we are in danger of misjudging their motivations or intentions. If you hold a perception about someone which is going to influence a decision that affects them, check that your assumptions are right before it's too late to change or reverse your decision.

✗ You forget the value of diversity

We tend to look for similarities in people so that we can make connections with them easily; but this undermines the creative potential of a diverse group. Try being aware of the different qualities and attributes that a diverse team brings to a decision, and deliberately canvass ideas and celebrate creative solutions.

STEPS TO SUCCESS

✔ Discovering a new approach to old problems can revitalise your working life.

✔ Talk to colleagues to canvass their ideas.

✔ Make use of a variety of tried and tested decision-making techniques.

✔ Get into the habit of looking at issues from different perspectives.

✔ Ask someone new to the situation for their immediate response—it could give you the key you need to make the right decision.

✔ Don't be taken by surprise; anticipate the potential fall-out from your decision.

Useful links

MindTools.com:
www.mindtools.com
The Mind Gym:
www.themindgym.com

Asking the right questions

Asking questions is something we learn to do as children. When we're learning about the world, we are curious, interested, and hungry for information. However, when young we are often discouraged from asking questions by irritable retorts from adults who don't have time to explain. When we go to school we're encouraged to provide the 'right' answers, and when we're teenagers we always seem to be asking the 'wrong' questions – questions to which the answer is often 'No!' So we enter our adult years without having perfected this art which can help 'open up' the world to us.

Asking a carefully positioned and accurate question—the 'right' question—can be extremely illuminating and give us the information we need to make accurate judgements and good decisions. This chapter will help you to do just that.

Step one: Know the different types of question

Before you start thinking about how you should ask a question, think about what you are asking the question for. Different kinds of question yield different results, so it's important to know what you need from your answer. There are several different types of question:

✔ Closed questions

Closed questions prompt an 'either/or' answer, for example 'Yes/No', 'Three/Four', 'Green/Blue'. These are unambiguous answers that provide information. They do not open up conversations or lead to a discussion, but they are useful for clarifying a situation or to confirm understanding of a more in-depth response to a question.

TOP TIP

If you come into contact with someone who 'waffles', take the lead and ask a series of closed questions to clarify the points that they are trying to make. You could open with 'Can I just check that I've understood the key points?' and then ask some clarifying closed questions.

✔ Open questions

Open questions lead to an exploration of the other person's views and opinions. They bring in a great deal of information and are often used in exploratory conversations and philosophical discussions. Open questions often require imaginative responses and may be 'left in the air', either for dramatic effect or to stimulate deeper consideration.

Open questions are also used in coaching conversations which are designed to bring the 'coachee's' ideas and natural wisdom to the surface. They help them to hear themselves work something out that they may not have thought about before. Open questions bring into the open what would otherwise remain tacit. They are the 'Tell me more' questions:

- 'Who . . .?'
- 'What . . .?'
- 'Where . . .?'
- 'When . . .?'
- 'Why . . .?'
- 'How . . .?'

✔ Factual questions

Factual questions are asked when information is needed on a topic where there is a consensus of opinion or belief; when meaning is shared by a wider community—of scientists, for instance.

TOP TIP
If you don't know who to ask for specific kinds of information, find someone who you think has a wide network and a clear understanding of the situation and ask for their opinion. If you always end such conversations by asking, 'Who else should I be talking to?', you'll gain access to a wider network of informed people.

✔ **Naïve questions**

Naïve or childlike questions are often asked to bring the core of an issue to the surface. They are often ignored because they can disturb the equilibrium. However, the more they are ignored, the greater the collusion of ignorance; it's important to appreciate how useful they can be. Typically, the naïve questioner asks 'Why?' followed by another 'Why?' and yet another 'Why?'!

TOP TIP
If someone starts giving you unnecessary information when they are answering one of your questions, you may need to be more assertive. Find the chance to interject with a comment like: 'That's very interesting, but I wonder if I could direct you back to . . .'

✔ Questions that pass information

In some circumstances, questions can be used to relay information. The job interview is a good opportunity for this. If you aren't being asked questions that allow you to show yourself in a good light, you may want to ask a question that prompts a follow-up question from your interviewer. This is also a useful technique if you're in a meeting or trying to influence the outcome of a negotiation. An example of such a question could be: 'Would you like to know about the experience I had working in China?'

✔ Provocative questions

These questions can be used to stir up a debate. An example of a provocative question is 'So you really think child labour is OK?' These types of question are generally values-based, and seek a closed answer on one level but warrant debate on another. We may see these questions in political debate when someone wants to reveal a hidden motivation for a certain behaviour or decision. Provocative questions should be used carefully because they often result in heated debate, if not an all-out argument!

✔ Leading questions

Leading questions imply a certain answer before the respondent has given it – for instance, 'When did you start embezzling from your company?' We often see leading questions used in television interviews or in court hearings where witnesses are being examined by the prosecution.

✓ Clarifying questions

These types of question are used to check that you have understood someone's response properly. You can ask questions such as 'Did you mean. . .?' and follow up with your interpretation of what they've said. If you'd like to understand their motivations for giving a particular response, you could say, 'Would you explain how you reached this conclusion?'

TOP TIP
Often, something that someone says in a meeting triggers a series of thoughts that distract us. If this happens to you, you could ask for a summary of the points that have been made so far, in order to confirm your understanding. Or you could simply admit that a point was so interesting that you followed it in your mind and lost the thread of the discussion! Most people can identify with this and are happy to go back over the key points.

Step two: Ask the right questions

✓ Be clear about why you are asking the question. What kind of information do you need to help you to make your decision?

✓ Select the type of question that fits your purpose—or decide on the sequence of the questions you need to ask. You may begin with a closed question and then

---

open up the conversation to be more exploratory. An example is 'Do you think we should rebrand our products? . . . Why do you think this is important?'

✔ Think about the context. Are your surroundings conducive to your purpose? Do you need privacy or are you able to pose your question in an open forum where opinion can be shared? You don't want to make the respondent feel uncomfortable and get an incomplete or ill-thought-through response as a result.

✔ Ask one question at a time. It's very tempting to ask multiple questions but this only confuses the respondent. They may not know which question to answer first, and in answering one of the questions they may forget to answer the other. An example of a multiple question is: 'Did you feel undermined and how would you have preferred to have been addressed?'

✔ Be clear. Try to be as unambiguous as possible by posing your question precisely. Some people take an age to ask a question, perhaps because they are unsure of whether or how they should ask it. When this happens, it's difficult to know exactly what the question is because there's so much 'waffle'.

✔ You can get different responses depending on the timing of your question. Think about your conversation as a drama and, if appropriate, try to time your question so that it has the greatest chance of yielding the information you need—or of creating the most impact.

Step three: Listen to the answers!

If you ask the 'right' questions, make sure you listen to the answers! If you think you know how someone is going to respond to you, you'll have a tendency to filter out any information that goes against your expectations. Try to withhold any comments or subsequent questions until you have fully heard, and digested, what is being said. Also, don't finish other people's sentences for them. It's rude and will infuriate them.

Common mistakes

✗ **You fudge your question and get an uninformative response**

This can happen if you are unsure of the person or the situation. Try to be clear in your own mind before asking the question. Think about the circumstances, the environment, and the type of question that would give you the information you need.

✗ **You think you know what the person is going to say so don't listen to their response**

This happens all too often. If you ask a question, it's important that you listen to the answer. Suspend judgement and allow other people to finish what they're saying before you ask any secondary questions. You could also repeat what they have said back to them so that they know you have been listening properly, and can clarify any points you may have misunderstood. An example is 'So the product will be ready a month early?'

✗ You argue

Don't go there. If you don't hear what you want to hear, it doesn't mean that the other person is wrong. Nor does it mean that he or she needs persuading that they are wrong. Sometimes we just have to accept that other people see the world differently from us—or maybe that we are ourselves wrong!

✗ You don't ask a question because you feel that you should know the answer

This can lead you into deep water. It's better to look foolish for a few minutes than to make a crass mistake because you didn't dare ask the question. There will probably be other people who are grateful that you've asked.

STEPS TO SUCCESS

✔ Don't be afraid to ask questions. It's far better to take the time to understand the situation than to muddle through and risk making the wrong decision.

✔ Think about the best question for your purpose.

✔ If you're short of time, closed questions may be the best approach.

✔ Open questions can lead to an enlightening discussion.

✔ If you have time, repeat your question over to yourself before you ask it to check that it won't get people's backs up—unless you want it to!

✔ Make sure you pick the right time to ask your questions. Is the context right? Is the person you need to speak to busy or irritable? If so, it may be worth trying them at another time—if your deadline allows.

Useful links

Steve Pavlina, Personal Development for Smart People:
www.stevepavlina.com/blog/2006/02/asking-the-right-questions
American Speech-Language-Hearing Association, 'Asking the Right Questions in the Right Ways':
www.asha.org/about/publications/leader-online/archives/2003/q2/f030429b.htm

Using proven problem-solving techniques

We all possess problem-solving skills to some degree or another. However, as our experience builds, our problem-solving skills tend to become less imaginative and we tend to resort to default solutions. Using favoured tried and tested approaches is all very well, but sometimes the context changes, old solutions become redundant, and new options become available. To give yourself the best chance of making a good decision, it's important to keep re-examining your circumstances and evolving new solutions to potential problems.

The techniques in this chapter will help you to reframe your problem and discover creative solutions that you may not have thought of before. Even if some of the solutions seem wacky at first, they are valuable nonetheless; their viability may well change over time as other developments influence the situation. Think beyond the immediate problem and imagine the potential knock-on effects. Solutions that affect the wider environment could pay unexpected dividends.

Step one: Work out the best approach

Knowing how to tackle a problem is always a challenge. Think about your usual approach. Do you work backwards from the problem in order to find the possible cause, or do you work forward from the problem and assume that the cause will remain in place? Find a technique that fits in with your natural analytical or creative style and follow it through, analysing your thought processes as you go. Once you're aware of your 'comfort zone', you can branch out and try other techniques such as those described below.

TOP TIP

Weaning ourselves off our usual habits is difficult, but trial and error is as good a way as any to break our habitual pattern. By removing yourself from your comfort zone you may well surprise yourself with the innovative solutions you come up with.

It doesn't matter which technique you adopt as long you start thinking about the problem differently. Find an approach that fits in with the time and resources available. If you're very logical, you might like to use a more analytical technique such as research and analogy (see step four). If you are more creative, try using one of the brainstorming or lateral thinking techniques described in steps two and three.

Step two: Brainstorm

Brainstorming is a technique that brings together a group of people to focus on a particular issue or problem. It's a great way of generating new ideas by using the collective creative resources of those who may not— arguably *should* not—be familiar with the technicalities of the problem. Bear in mind, though, that it's not a random activity. It is a structured process that puts the richness of diverse thinking to good use. To ensure that a useful structure is in place, brainstorming sessions should be chaired and records should be kept of any output. Below is a template for the process:

1 **Define the situation and agree the desired outcome.** Make sure everyone knows what the problem is and what needs to be achieved in the time allotted.

2 **Encourage everyone's participation.** Agree that all ideas should be considered positively and that no-one will be shot down for being radical or ridiculous.

3 **Set a time limit.** This is not an endless exploration. Usually, the best ideas come early, so set a limit to the time spent brainstorming or keep in touch with the group's energy and bring the session to a close when it runs low.

4 **Collect all ideas for later discussion.** Capture everything. Don't filter at this stage; that comes later.

5 **Look for patterns and common themes in the ideas generated.** You may be able to put several ideas into the same category or create clusters of related ideas. This begins to make the output more manageable.

6 **Begin the refining and selection process.** Discuss in what circumstances the ideas could be adopted, and what's needed to make them work.

7 **Create a list of top options.** Assign people to develop these ideas further and evaluate their viability.

8 **Review and follow up.** Ensure that everyone knows the outcome so that they can feel valued for their contribution.

TOP TIP
It might be helpful to have someone in your brainstorming group who knows nothing about the problem or situation. A bit of distance can be a huge help.

Step three: Try role-play

If you're struggling with a problem, it might help to observe someone else solving it who is not constrained by your knowledge about the subject. Although the thought of role-play fills many people with dread, it can be a very powerful way of looking at things from a completely different perspective and exploring a problem at considerable depth.

First, brief your role-play partner about your problem and explain where you would like to get to by the end of the exercise. Take the role of coach for the rest of the exercise:

1 **Get your 'coachee' to explain what the goal is.** This will reassure you that they have understood the problem and the point of the exercise.

2 **Ask them to focus on the present.** What's the current situation and what barriers or obstacles exist to prevent them from finding a novel solution? (This is not to be negative, but hearing them explore the situation may throw light on a different way of looking at things.)

3 **Facilitate a brainstorming session.** Ask them 'What ideas have you got for a solution?', 'What would be the ideal outcome?', 'What's preventing this from occurring?', 'What could you do about this?', and so on. This is the bread and butter of the role-play. You may be very surprised to hear what ideas they have. Don't forget to take notes.

4 **Ask them to put together an action plan.** They should sort out what they see as the priorities and tell you what needs to be done in order to implement their solution.

Stay in role for the duration of the exercise and resist the temptation to criticise their suggestions. Instead, if they suggest something that you think won't work, ask them, 'What needs to be done to make this succeed?' Or 'What alternative ideas can you come up with?'

You will be surprised how inventive people can be when their perspective isn't clouded by past experiences of a situation.

The 'Silent Observer' is another form of role-play that involves two people in discussion about the problem. You, the problem holder, are the (restrained) observer. Again, it is important not to interrupt the flow with countering comments. During this exercise, you merely observe and record two people in dialogue looking at things from a fresh perspective.

Step four: Research and analogy

This is a more logical technique that may suit people who are not comfortable with intuitive creativity. It focuses on the problem directly and seeks others' solutions. Ask yourself the following questions:

✔ 'Who else may have encountered this problem?'

✔ 'Who has solved this problem successfully in the past?'

✔ 'What else does this problem look like?'

By asking yourself these questions and working out what has been done before, you will be able to find a more precise solution.

You could also think about the nature of the problem and consider whether it might occur in a similar form but in a different context. By asking yourself the question 'What else could this problem look like?' you may find that you venture into new territory where a solution is equally applicable to your situation.

TOP TIP
It's quite possible to streamline your chosen approach so that you find a good solution without taking endless time over it. Be clear about your time and resource limitations and find an approach that works well for you. You'll find that it pays dividends as you gain more experience.

Step five: Challenging assumptions

Our assumptions are so ingrained that we often forget to question them. Yet sometimes our assumptions about a particular problem or situation are no longer valid because the context has changed—for example, as a result of advances in technology and design. As assumptions are an intrinsic part of the way we view the world, we need to take deliberate steps to expose them. The first step, therefore, in challenging assumptions is to articulate them. This can be done by getting someone to ask us directly about our assumptions. If they continue to probe, they will reveal our core assumption, which may well sit at odds with the desired outcome. We can then ask, 'Is the assumption relevant or should it be reconsidered?' and 'Is it helpful in this situation to hold this assumption?'

Once it has been revealed, we can look at the nature of the assumption. What's limiting our pool of solutions? Is it:

- an assumption about the time available?
- an assumption about the cost?
- an assumption that the resources won't be made available to us?
- an assumption that our suggestions won't be politically acceptable?
- an underestimation of our skills and/or knowledge?
- an assumption that there are other barriers to implementing our solution?

TOP TIP

If you've seen most of the problems before, your experience will be very useful in appraising the results of decisions made using some of the proven techniques. But don't get stuck in a rut. Most sectors

---

**are conducting their business in a
rapidly changing environment. These
changing dynamics are bound to
have an impact at all levels. Try
something different and see
where it takes you.**

Once you have a list of assumptions underpinning the
'impossibility' of a novel solution, try looking at the problem
from a position where your assumptions don't hold and see
where this leads you. Once you reveal what you believe to be
the constraints behind a novel solution, you can start
challenging and overcoming them.

Common mistakes

✗ You don't put boundaries around your problem-solving activities

Don't get overwhelmed with ideas that you then find
difficult to sift through and sort out. Remember to focus
on one technique at a time and put some constraints
around the time you spend on it. Once you have a pool of
ideas, move on to the next stage. You can always return
to the ideas generation stage if you don't find a viable
solution.

✗ You think that you have to know all the answers

Sometimes people feel that it's weak to admit that they
have run out of ideas, but engaging others in problem-

solving activities is a good way of generating ideas which can add real value. Not only is this good for the business, but it will also show you in a better light than if you try to struggle through on your own.

✗ You feel that activities such as brainstorming are a waste of time

They can be very helpful in the right context. Such activities have a double advantage: not only do they help to find a way out of a problem, but they can also provide team-building benefits. The shared experience doesn't stop at the end of the brainstorming session; it will oil the wheels of your professional network, and will engender an atmosphere of creativity and co-operation.

STEPS TO SUCCESS

✔ Re-evaluate the situation regularly and assess whether your favoured solutions are still valid.

✔ Don't get stuck in a rut: try new ways of doing things.

✔ Remember that there's always more than one way of solving a problem.

✔ Be open to the unexpected.

✔ Make a point of trying out new techniques and seeing where they take you.

✔ Examine other people's approaches carefully; they may well be enlightening.

✔ Look at the wider implications of your decision.

Useful links

Basic guidelines for problem solving and decision making:
www.managementhelp.org/prsn_prd/prb_bsc.htm
MindTools:
www.mindtools.com/pages/main/newMN_TMC.htm

Making good decisions under pressure

When we're called on to make decisions under pressure, we often worry that we'll make the wrong choice, and that it will come back to haunt us. Most of us prefer to have enough time to analyse the situation and consider the alternatives. When time is tight, however, we don't have this luxury.

That said, some of the best decisions we make are the ones we make when we're up against it. Pressure can result in focused attention and logical reasoning. It forces us to sort the relevant factors from the irrelevant and can result in clear thinking and clear priorities. If you follow the advice in this book, you'll develop good decision-making habits. Combined with the advice in this chapter, these will stand you in good stead when you are put under pressure and need to focus on making the right decision.

Step one: Know the tools

Decision making is not something that we are all naturally good at, but it *is* something we can learn. As we saw in the earlier chapters, there are many tools that can help in the decision-making process. However, if these techniques aren't moderated by experience and a feeling for what will work and what won't, they can be clumsy.

TOP TIP

If you tend to panic when put under pressure to make a decision, it's probably because you're running through all the disaster scenarios that may arise if you make the wrong decision. This clouds your thinking and adds yet more pressure. Focus on the relevant information, and put the rest to the back of your mind. Should you wish, you can mull it over later—but for now you need to prioritise and focus on the key factors.

If you're under pressure to make a decision, you won't have time to use the approaches mentioned earlier. Instead, you will be forced into being reactive and to draw upon your intuition. Some people seem to be fortunate enough to have a good feel for what needs to be done—but if you scratch the surface, you'll probably find that they have drawn from their experience and memories of what has worked in the past and what hasn't.

'Good' decisions are usually made as a result of unpressured analysis. If you're in a job where you might have to make decisions under pressure, you would do well to look ahead and go through likely decisions 'virtually' before they need to be made. Doing this means that even if you don't meet the exact situation, you will already have rehearsed

---

a number of different scenarios, so your thinking will be faster, clearer, and more readily accessible.

Step two: Do a risk analysis in advance

If you don't have extensive experience, by thinking ahead you will protect yourself from serious errors when making decisions under pressure. This is what the emergency services do when they role-play serious situations or crises. Everything is enacted as if it is really happening, so that the parties involved can practise making good decisions under pressure. Then, when the situation occurs in reality, they are able to make decisions rapidly and effectively.

Think through a series of 'disaster scenarios' and come to some conclusions about what you'd do if any of them actually happened. This is not a negative activity and, with a bit of luck, none of the situations you envisage will come about. However, if they do, you will already have been through the thought processes in your mind and will be able to access them quickly. Here's a checklist for conducting a risk analysis:

1 Speculate on the threats. These include financial, technical, operational, and human. Ask yourself 'What if. . .' until you have exhausted all possible scenarios.

2 Measure the likelihood of the risk occurring. Think about the combination of the cost and the probability of its happening. By doing this, you will be able to

highlight the worst-case scenario and consider this
first.

3 Start with the most critical risk and think through the
different ways in which you could address it. By going
through this exercise before the risk occurs, you may be
able to devise a contingency plan, or even eliminate the
risk altogether.

4 Make contact with anyone who's likely to be involved
and inform them of any procedures they need to
apply or approaches that they need to take in order
to manage the situation effectively. If everyone is
pre-warned, informed of their role, and kept briefed
about the probability of something occurring, they
will be able to help you move swiftly when you
have to.

Step three: Understand the situation

When something happens that requires your urgent
attention, try not to jump to conclusions or act in a way
that reflects your fears rather than what is actually going
on. Breathe deeply a couple of times, give yourself time to
appraise the situation, then decide which of the scenarios
you have already thought through most closely matches
what has happened. It's difficult to predict a situation
precisely, so be prepared to 'mix and match' your
prepared responses so that they meet the demands of the
situation.

Step four: Sort out the relevant from the irrelevant facts

We often get overwhelmed by information in crisis
situations—but there are usually only one or two important
facts on which the decision rests. Don't get waylaid by
factors that are irrelevant to the current decision. Discard any
information that is clouding your judgement and address it
later. By asking yourself, 'Is this critical now?' you will be
able to reject elements of the situation that don't warrant
urgent attention.

> **good communication is vital—especially if
> your decision has an impact on others. It
> would be a shame to be called to account for a
> decision you made and to have to admit you
> were pressured to do so by someone else!**

Step five: Apply weightings

It sometimes helps if you put scores or weightings on the
options that are available to you so that you can see clearly
which are the most suitable decisions. If the situation is
highly pressured you may have to do this in your head—but
this activity will focus your mind and help you to make good
decisions. If you make a habit of this, as you become more
experienced you'll find that you begin to do it almost without
thinking.

Step six: Talk your decision through
with someone

To make sure you haven't missed anything in your rush,
check your logic by talking things through with a trusted or
experienced colleague. Just hearing yourself talk about it
could further clarify your rationale for making a decision.

Remember that a 'good' decision doesn't necessarily
guarantee a satisfactory outcome. Sometimes, even when

we have gone through a careful decision-making process to make what we believe to be a good decision, it turns sour. Following the advice in this book to the letter won't protect you from failure; all you can do is stack up the odds in your favour and hope that you aren't sabotaged by chance or circumstance. As you become more experienced, though, your skills will develop and you will become more confident in your choices.

Common mistakes

✗ You become overwhelmed by the weight of the responsibility

If you allow yourself to become overwhelmed, your logic will become clouded and your decision-making ability will be compromised. No matter what the time pressures are, make sure that you listen attentively and collect all the information available before moving into decision-making mode. This will enable you to remain clear-headed as you sift through the facts and find out what's *really* going on. Many mistakes are made when people assume they know what's happening and stop seeing and hearing what's going on around them. It's well known that we often see and hear what we expect to see and hear!

✗ You don't brief people properly

Not briefing people properly about what's expected of them can slow things down and will increase the pressure on anyone involved in the situation—including yourself. If you're making rapid decisions under pressure, the last thing you want is people asking what they should be doing or how they should be doing it.

✗ You get stuck in irrelevant detail

This is one of the common barriers to making good decisions. Although it's true that the devil is in the detail, if the detail isn't immediately relevant it should be set aside for the time being. Try to eliminate as many irrelevancies as possible so that you can see to the heart of the issue. This will help you focus on what needs to be done and what decisions need to be taken.

✗ You take it all on yourself

Don't hold back for the sake of your pride: ask someone who's more experienced than you and get them to talk you through the rationale for the recommendations they make. This will help you to learn the ropes so that you are able to use your new experience next time.

STEPS TO SUCCESS

✔ Think ahead and rehearse possible scenarios *before* they happen.

✔ Remember that pressure isn't always a bad thing: it can force you to think things through more clearly and efficiently.

✔ Focus on what is immediately relevant to the decision.

✔ Even when short of time you should analyse your assumptions: don't jump to conclusions.

✔ When you're under pressure, it's even more important that you 'check in' with a trusted colleague to make sure that you haven't missed anything crucial.

Useful links

MindTools.com, 'How to make better decisions':
www.mindtools.com/pages/main/newMN_TED.htm
MindTools.com, 'Making good decisions under pressure':
www.mindtools.com/pages/article/newTED_99.htm
Free online tools to help decision making under pressure:
www.rfp-templates.com/search/for/Free-Online-Tools-to-Help-Decision-Making-Under-Pressure.html

Conducting a cost/benefit analysis

Whether you are making a major decision or pitching for a major project, a cost/benefit analysis could be invaluable. When you have spent time and effort coming up with the idea for a new project or initiative, before you decide whether to take it to the next stage it's important to establish whether or not it is viable. In a cost/benefit analysis every aspect of the project is given a financial value, the costs and benefits are compared, and it's generally found to be viable if the benefits outweigh the costs.

While the process sounds extremely subjective, cost/benefit analyses can actually take into account qualitative value, so won't necessarily factor out 'good' ideas that don't have an immediately apparent financial return. A major bonus of using this type of analysis is that it enables you to frame an argument in financial terms—which is generally the basis for getting approval for any project or initiative.

Step one: Know the pros and cons of a cost/benefit analysis

Because the exact financial value of each potential expenditure and reward can be debatable, this approach is subjective to a certain degree. It is therefore helpful to know what level of accuracy you can expect. Before you do a cost/benefit analysis, make sure that it's the right tool for the job by considering the advantages and disadvantages of the technique.

Advantages

- A cost/benefit analysis puts a financial value on the viability of a project or initiative so that a 'go/no-go' decision can be made.
- Many aspects of a project or initiative have to be considered in this type of analysis. Considering them will help you to learn more about the proposal and raise issues that had not been thought of. It can also mean that roles and responsibilities can be allocated more effectively should the project get the green light.
- Unexpected costs may be brought to light, which helps prevent expensive mistakes from being made.
- The break-even point or payback period of the project can be identified.
- It's very difficult to argue against a robust cost/benefit analysis, so it can help you to persuade people who are unsure about it, or for whom it's not a 'pet' project.

Disadvantages

- Some people consider a cost/benefit analysis to be over-simplistic.
- Cost/benefit analyses are peppered with assumptions and subjective measures which may distort the 'real' value of the project. Simply setting different boundaries may cause the viability of a project to change dramatically.
- Some of the costs and benefits of a project are non-tangible, so a (potentially contentious) value will need to be placed on these.
- Many of the longer-term costs and benefits are estimated, which can result in an inaccurate measure of the project's value.
- 'Worthy' projects may be vetoed on the basis of their costs, or cheapened to make them viable.

TOP TIP
Many high-profile projects have proven to cost double, triple, or quadruple the amount used in the cost/benefit calculation. Bearing in mind the potential for error, you should always allow for higher costs than expected.

Step two: Define the perspective, boundaries, and timelines

The more you know about the timeline and scope of the project, the better you will be at estimating the costs and benefits. A good way of learning more about a project is to look at it from different points of view. To help you do this, follow the guidance in chapter 2—but remember that mixing different viewpoints can lead to a confused analysis. Don't let your research get out of control and distract you from the matter at hand. Keep clear about why you are doing the project and who you are doing it for.

Step three: Assign the costs

Identify and assign all the costs that are likely to be incurred on the project. These include not just the costs of the materials or resources required (the variable costs) but also, for instance, the costs of employing people (the direct costs) and of running the office (the overheads). You may find that in order to get a more accurate picture of the costs and benefits, you will need to extend the scope of your analysis to include any knock-on costs. For instance, you might be able to add a new product to your production line without incurring punitive costs, but the costs of packaging, marketing, or distribution might turn out to be prohibitive.

✔ Be clear about the assumptions you're making when calculating costs, whether they are tangible or intangible.

Also, make sure that you factor in ongoing costs as well as start-up costs. Costs have a habit of reoccurring when you least expect them!

TOP TIP
There are some occasions when it would be politically unacceptable not to undertake a particular project or programme. In these instances, a cost/benefit analysis may serve to ensure that the project is run as efficiently as possible, with careful cost control.

Step four: Assign monetary values to the benefits

Some outputs will have a definite value, but there are also likely to be intangible benefits. Again, this is where you need to make assumptions and use the 'best estimate'. When the cost/benefit analysis is discussed and the proposal considered, this is where many of the decision-makers will focus their arguments.

TOP TIP
If you're having difficulty putting a value on a
non-tangible aspect of a project or initiative,
try looking at what the cost would be if you
didn't implement it. This gives you an idea of
its worth.

Step five: Consider the longer-term effects

If the project is long term, you will need to calculate its future value in today's terms—its net present value (NPV). The NPV is the sum of the initial project cost plus the **present value** of expected future cash-flows. The 'present value' is the current value of any future costs and benefits, adjusted to allow for inflation and/or interest. You should also think about the **opportunity costs**. These are the costs of *not* proceeding with the project or of allocating the funds elsewhere. Once you have done this, you need to think about what **rate of return** would be possible if the money were invested differently.

When looking at time-related costs, you have to look not only at the likely effects of time on the value of money—such as inflation—but also at the depreciation of any related capital assets.

TOP TIP

If the costs outweigh the benefits but you still feel that the project is vital to the business, calculating the NPV could be extremely useful for you. By looking at the long-term effects of the project you may be able to show it in a more favourable financial light.

If the NPV exceeds the opportunity costs, then the project should be seriously considered.

Step six: Be aware of your assumptions

Make sure that you are aware of the assumptions you've made to arrive at all the figures you have used in your cost/benefit analysis. These can be the Achilles heel of any analysis and will be subject to scrutiny if the project or initiative is contentious.

TOP TIP

Try to find similar projects that have been approved in your organisation and look at what assumptions have been made. You may also find something that you can use in your own analysis that will help weight your argument favourably. It's much harder to reject a project if the basis on which it has been analysed is similar to that for one which has already been accepted.

As there are so many variables to take into account, many of which are out of your control, it's important to remember that any longer-term predictions carry a higher level of uncertainty. Consult as widely as you can with people who you think have a good grasp of the patterns and trends so that you can get the best idea possible of what the future will bring. You will never be 100 per cent correct but at least you'll be stacking the odds in your favour. Do a reality check on your analysis, but also be aware of your gut feelings. Ask yourself, 'Am I being realistic?' and 'Am I becoming too emotionally committed to a particular outcome?' You should know whether your desired outcome is colouring your cost or benefit arguments.

Having done a cost/benefit analysis, remember to check the prospective project's viability or desirability from a wider perspective. For instance, if the project veers away from your core business there are likely to be knock-on implications. You should also take into account any associated organisational, cultural, or political issues.

Common mistakes

✗ You manipulate the data

This is a common mistake. If your heart is set on a project, you may be tempted to 'massage' the figures so that it looks more desirable. You may change your assumptions, underestimate the set-up costs, or overestimate the value of the benefits. This may lead to a positive decision but, in the long term, the project is very unlikely to yield the predicted value.

✗ You focus on the short term

If you focus only on the immediate costs and benefits of implementing a project, a misleading picture will emerge. It's important to factor in the opportunity costs (the costs of *not* doing a project, or of doing a different project), as this may show the project in a completely different light.

✗ You don't examine your assumptions

If you have an interest in gaining a particular outcome, you may highlight certain costs or benefits to make your proposal more convincing. Using the cost/benefit analysis as a selling tool is all very well as long as it doesn't land you in hot water. Use it to test your own assumptions and undertake the analysis process rigorously and truthfully.

STEPS TO SUCCESS

✔ Whether you are making decisions based on someone else's cost/benefit analysis or doing one yourself, double-check that nothing crucial has been missed out, on either the cost side or the benefits side.

✔ Always be aware of any assumptions made. Ask several people to check them, to make sure that they stand up to scrutiny.

✔ Re-examine all estimates several times: the analysis is only as accurate as the estimates on which it's based.

✔ Make sure that allowance has been made for extra contingency costs.

✔ Although cost/benefit analyses are time-consuming, remember that the best way of getting management buy-in is to present your case from a financial perspective.

✔ Keep an eye on the long term: factor in ongoing costs and benefits.

Useful links

Wikipedia:
http://en.wikipedia.org/wiki/Cost-benefit_analysis
MindTools.com:
www.mindtools.com/pages/article/newTED_08.htm
An introduction to cost/benefit analysis:
www.sjsu.edu/faculty/watkins/cba.htm

Avoiding procrastination

It's no use having the tools if you don't use them! Procrastination in the workplace can result in decisions not being made and actions not being taken, and can cause a frustrating bottleneck that disrupts the effectiveness of a team. As it can be a significant barrier to progress, it's important that it's recognised and dealt with as soon as possible.

Procrastination can be done collectively by a group of people who consistently fail to come to an agreement, or it can be done individually. 'Perfectionists' often lack confidence when making decisions, and may not be happy with the options available. They may overcomplicate matters and come up against seemingly irresolvable dead ends. They often focus on what might go wrong and are reluctant to take risks or settle for 'more or less' solutions.

In this chapter we look at ways in which you can address and avoid procrastination, both in general and when making decisions.

Step one: Know when and why you're procrastinating

As we have seen, good decisions have a better chance of being made when the circumstances surrounding them have been properly analysed and understood, and all the options have been considered and appraised. However, doing this obsessively can result in procrastination and poor decisions.

Procrastination is behavioural, and has a number of possible causes:

■ **Fear of failure.** Procrastinators often feel that they're being watched, and have a fear of 'getting it wrong' and being humiliated. This fear may be rooted in low self-confidence, lack of clarity about the task, or a lack of knowledge or experience. When people procrastinate, it can be because they doubt their ability to make a decision or take an action which will lead to a satisfactory outcome. So they put off the hour when they will have to act, thereby avoiding a public failure.

■ **A drive for perfection.** Sometimes procrastinators are driven by the need to achieve 'perfect' solutions. Nothing pleases perfectionists. They feel that there's always an improvement to be made, so are continually 'tweaking', and as a result can fail to achieve anything definite.

- **Conflicting values or priorities.** If someone is asked to work on something that goes against their belief system or that is not high on their list of priorities, they may put it off repeatedly until it is impossible to avoid it any longer. This can be really frustrating for those whose activities depend upon delivery from the procrastinator.

- **Political sabotage.** Sometimes procrastination is a deliberate act of sabotage which may be being used for political purposes. If someone blocks progress by failing to play their part, they may achieve something that they value more highly—or avoid something that they don't want to happen. Indeed, sometimes procrastinators are so effective at blocking that the issue goes away altogether!

TOP TIP

If you find yourself carrying out activities that don't contribute to the achievement of your goals, you may well be procrastinating. We often distract ourselves with other things when we don't really want to get down to something that is 'too hard', 'too boring', or 'too complicated'.

Step two: Identify the goal you want to reach (or the one you're struggling to reach)

Be clear about what you want to achieve and what it would look and feel like once you have achieved it. This helps you to get a concrete sense of where you are going and gives you a tangible measure of success. Sometimes we procrastinate because we're unsure of the end goal. If you can't get a clear idea of this on your own, discuss it with someone else who is involved; this should help you to focus on what needs to be done.

Step three: Understand the current situation

Look at where you are now. What's going on for you? What are the barriers to your progress? Are they real or imaginary? See if you can diagnose the root of your reluctance to make a decision or take action. Once you understand where the stumbling blocks are, you'll be in a better position to overcome them. If you feel that you don't have enough knowledge or experience, ask for support. If resources are limited, take the initiative by looking for additional resources and presenting the case for their provision.

TOP TIP
It's very difficult to make decisions when you're unsure where the boundaries to your authority lie. If you feel that this is the cause of your procrastination, clarify things with your line manager. Ask for a meeting to discuss this and take some examples to him or her so that you can determine your decision-making authority.

Step four: Break things down into manageable pieces

Sometimes we're overwhelmed by the enormous implications of a decision, project, or task. If you break it down into its constituent parts, it is often easier to see a way through. One step at a time always gets you there eventually.

Analysing your project to-do list in this way may also enable you to see which jobs are getting in the way. You can eliminate or delegate them, to give you a chance to focus your mind and get on with things.

TOP TIP

It's very difficult to motivate someone to meet your needs if they can't see the consequences of their behaviour. If your work is being held up by a procrastinator, try talking to him or her and explaining how their procrastination affects your workload. You could ask them if there's anything you could do to help them. Regular (gentle!) reminders could help them to concentrate on what needs to be done.

Step five: Create a plan

Once you have seen what progress can be made by taking small steps, put some timelines and deadlines together to create a plan. This will focus your attention and provide the necessary perspective to help you make steady progress. Focus on one task or issue at a time and make sure that you complete each one as you go. This means that even if you haven't yet reached your goal, you can still report on progress—which is much more positive than being perpetually stuck in procrastination and denial.

Step six: Celebrate your successes

Make sure you take note of your own achievements, and perhaps let others know too. Try not to over-reach yourself by seeking to achieve too much in one go; divide up your energy according to how much you have to devote to each task or decision, and take time out to attend to other activities that will refresh your concentration.

Procrastinators often get stuck in a vicious cycle. Perhaps for one of the reasons above, they put off a decision or action, which then creates more pressure on them to make a decision or take an action, which further paralyses their ability to make a decision or take an action! And so it goes on until they are in a corner, under pressure, with nowhere to go. Breaking out of this cycle is therefore important if you are to stop procrastinating.

Common mistakes

✗ You convince yourself that you're more efficient when you're under pressure

Chapter 5 offers advice on making decisions under pressure—but avoid it if you can. It can certainly focus the mind, but it does increase the risk of making an imprudent decision. If you are a procrastinator, try to set yourself an early deadline and give yourself an incentive for meeting it. You may win yourself a free weekend by making a decision or completing a task on Friday afternoon instead of having it hang over you until Monday.

✗ You let the pressure build until you're forced to make quick decisions and settle for less than satisfactory solutions

If this is your pattern, or you see it in others, try to spread out the pressure over time rather than letting it build until it is intolerable. If decisions are constantly being made under pressure, there is bound to be a higher than usual proportion of poor decisions.

✗ You procrastinate to gain a sense of power and control

This may be because you don't feel that your contribution is important or valued, or because you feel animosity towards someone. This is passive/aggressive behaviour and is not acceptable. You should recognise it and address it immediately.

✗ You think that if you ignore it, it will go away

This rarely happens. If this describes you, start with the easier decisions or tasks and build on them incrementally.

STEPS TO SUCCESS

✔ Recognise procrastination in yourself and others and address it quickly.

✔ Be self-aware: if you're procrastinating, look at your reasons for doing so.

✔ Be ready to compromise if necessary.

✔ Get a clear idea of your goals.

✔ If the decision is intimidating, tackle it one part at a time.

✔ If you're putting off a tricky decision, build your confidence by asking trusted colleagues for support.

Useful links

Stop procrastinating now!:

www.stopprocrastinatingnow.com

Personal development for smart people, 'Overcoming Procrastination':

www.stevepavlina.com/articles/overcoming-procrastination.htm

Procrastination Help:

www.procrastinationhelp.com

Getting your message across

So you've made your decision. The next step is to communicate that decision and its implications to your colleagues. This can sometimes be harder than making the decision in the first place, as people tend to be averse to change—especially if it means more work for them. If you're a new manager this may be even trickier, as you may feel that you don't yet have enough authority, and may be unsure of the best approach.

You need to ensure that your message is received in the way that you intend; simply telling people about the decision isn't enough. It's crucial that you bear in mind the wider picture and the values, beliefs, and motivations of the recipient(s). Being aware of and catering for these factors can enable you to tailor your communication so that you get your message across in the most effective way.

Step one: Understand the situation

Getting your message across eloquently and elegantly depends on your ability to read a situation accurately and to pick up on the social and political nuances at play among your colleagues. Some people are able to do this intuitively whilst others need some 'tools' to help them say the right thing at the right time. These may include organisational surveys which feed anonymous opinions back to the relevant people and raise issues that are important to employees without fear of repercussion. On the other hand, you may prefer to talk to a particularly politically astute or well-informed colleague to guide your approach.

Step two: Set the scene

If you're in a negotiation or meeting, it's a good idea to make clear to your audience why you're talking to them. By clearly stating your rationale you will help to address or sideline any alternative agendas or confusion. If you're working on any particular assumptions, make them clear and check that everyone else shares them. This will save a lot of time and potential crossed wires in the long run as it makes sure that everyone knows where they stand. Clarifying your aim will also help you refocus the meeting if things start to go awry.

Step three: Check your assumptions and explore the context

Sometimes you may need to make a strong personal connection with your audience before you deliver your message. To do this, you need to be aware of their concerns or expectations. Ask them what they think of the topic in question and find out about their related hopes and fears. Once you understand your audience's interests and motivations, you'll be able to work out the best way of communicating your decision. It's often a surprise to find that others don't share our assumptions, so making this initial check will make sure that you don't inadvertently press the wrong buttons.

TOP TIP

If you worry that you've made a decision that will make you appear inconsistent, the chances are that you will do. In this situation, honesty is the best policy. Address the apparent inconsistency directly and tell others how you'd feel if you saw someone else displaying this type of contradictory behaviour. This is a bold step, but it will make clear that you understand what others may be feeling, and will disarm potential critics. Having cleared the air, you can follow up by inviting others to tell you what they think, which allows you in turn to explain your reasoning rationally.

Step four: Meet the recipients on their own ground

Very often, messages don't get across well because the recipient can't relate to their content or purpose. If there's no point of identification or common interest between speaker and listener, there's no ground in which to root the message and as a result, its relevance gets lost. To get around this problem, it's a good idea to begin your speech with a phrase that tries to bridge the gap, such as 'As we're all aware . . .', or 'No doubt you've noticed that . . .'. Effective communicators take their audience's situation as their starting point and build towards the desired end point or outcome. You may need to do quite a lot of homework, both formally and informally, to be sure that you're properly informed of your audience's circumstances and views.

Step five: Use simple and elegant language

People who are experts in a particular field often baffle their audience with technical language or jargon on the assumption that it will have the same resonance with their audience as it does for them. Find out how familiar your audience is with the topic you're speaking on, and then adjust your vocabulary accordingly. Use plenty of examples, anecdotes, analogies, and metaphors if the audience isn't as 'techie' as you. Remember that you can also make your message clearer by using visual aids (such as PowerPoint or simple hand-outs). Humour and a touch of drama can sometimes help but it's best to use these sensitively and sparingly. Less is more.

Step six: Repeat key messages

Saying something once isn't enough. If your message is unpopular, you'll have to overcome people's natural inertia to it, and you can only do this by repeating it. Generally, people can take away about three key points from any communication. These three points may be represented in different ways so that all preferred styles of communication can be accommodated. In addition, they may be offered using different channels of communication so that the message is reinforced from many angles. For example, you could follow up a presentation by writing an article for a company newsletter or intranet. This will mean that no-one can avoid knowing about the decision, even if they don't agree with it!

TOP TIP

Remember that what you say and how you say it will be watched closely and discussed afterwards, so be sure that your behaviour supports your message. For example, you'll need to maintain eye contact with whoever you're speaking to as this emphasises the sincerity of your message. Remember that

---

some gestures are associated with lying and need to be avoided. They include hiding your mouth with your hand, touching your nose, blinking rapidly, and running a finger along the inside of your collar.

Step seven: Listen to others

Getting across your message successfully depends to a large extent on your ability to listen well to other people. We very often assume that we know what others are thinking and what they're about to say. However, these assumptions can 'deafen' us to what's *really* being said, and we end up as poor communicators as a result. Avoid this by listening properly to other people. Don't jump to conclusions or make snap judgments about their position, but instead respect where they're coming from and nurture a real desire to hear and be heard without the 'white noise' of misperception getting in the way.

TOP TIP
Many people resist change at first, so don't expect too much too soon. Connect with your team by showing you're aware of how they feel. For example, you could acknowledge that they've been under too much pressure lately, or that they've been asked to perform tasks that the team was

**not set up to do. You can then use this
common ground as the basis upon which
to explain the needs of the business and
how you propose to accommodate them
through structural change; a change that will
benefit all parties. Use your political
sensitivity and good judgement to decide how
much and how far you can go on this
occasion; you can always return to the
subject at a later date.**

Step eight: Address questions or concerns directly

In the same way that we must learn to hear our audience, we also have to help them hear us. Unless they're given an opportunity to have their concerns addressed honestly and constructively, they'll feel negative about the decision and may talk it down to those who haven't yet heard you explain yourself. Help your audience by being sure of both your subject and of your objectives in making the communication. Convey the necessary information accurately and remember that you have to seem convinced by it yourself if others are to share your belief. It's a good idea to close the communication 'loop' by asking your audience to summarise what they think you've said. This gives you a valuable opportunity to correct any misunderstandings and to run through your key points one more time. Getting colleagues 'on side' will enable them to act as another mouthpiece for your message.

Step nine: Summarise and confirm

There's an old adage about presentations that says 'tell them what you're going to tell them, tell them, then tell them what you've just told them'. Although this may sound like overkill, it's actually a valuable way of conveying messages in a straightforward and powerful way.

In short, use non-complex language to convey up to three points at a time repeatedly. Colour these points with examples, anecdotes, and analogies and be aware of how your decision is being received; if people look confused, adjust your style to explain things in plainer terms. If you see that people are straining to hear, speak louder. It's really important at all times to listen, observe, and respect your audience and their point of view, even if the latter is at odds with your own.

Common mistakes

✗ You over-do it

In our urgency to tell colleagues about a decision, it's tempting to rush in and speak without thinking things through. This will come across as arrogant and high-handed and will immediately set your audience against you. Rushing in like this is often based on a fear of failure and the thought that if we assert ourselves strongly enough, there'll be no room for disagreement or dissent. Wrong. In fact, if you do feel this fear, the best thing you can do is tread carefully. Show that you respect your audience, that you understand their situation and identify with it personally if you can. This will ease any likely resistance, especially if you ask them for their views and listen carefully to them.

✗ You undermine yourself by accident

We often believe that getting a message across is a content issue. However, it's not so much what you say that counts, but how you say it. Generally, people recognise authenticity and genuineness when they see it and unless you're in tune with your message and your audience, what you say will not be heard or received in the way you wish. To be in tune, you need to use your skills in active listening, body language, and assertiveness as well as believing in what you're saying.

✗ You don't allow enough time

Rushing your message when explaining a decision can leave people feeling bullied and demotivated. When you're planning and timing your communication, make sure you factor in some time for your audience to ask questions or raise concerns at the end. You need to put people at their ease so that they feel able to address what you've said. Don't be defensive if people ask you questions (remember that they're perfectly entitled to!), but try to use their point to build upon or illustrate another facet of your message.

STEPS TO SUCCESS

✔ Before telling people about your decision, plan your communication carefully.

✔ Make yourself aware of any office politics that may be affected by the decision.

✔ Listen to people's concerns and be prepared to talk though your processes in detail. If you have followed the advice in this book, they should stand up to scrutiny!

✔ Use clear language; don't blind your audience with science.

✔ Remember that getting defensive will do no-one any favours.

✔ If possible, tie your message in with your audience's values and motivations; explain how the decision will benefit them.

Useful links

1000ventures.com, 'Connecting with People':
www.1000ventures.com/business_guide/
crosscuttings/people_connecting.html
Mediate.com, 'Barriers to Everyday Communication':
www.mediate.com/articles/foster.cfm
Mindtools.com, 'Improve Your Communication Skills':
www.mindtools.com/page8.html

Where to find more help

**Good Question! The Art of Asking Questions
to Bring About Positive Change**
Judy Barber
Lean Marketing Press, 2005
288pp ISBN 1905430078

This book is a compilation of some of the favourite questions used by 28 of the sharpest minds in business and personal development today. It will help you to build your repertoire of good questions, enabling you to have conversations which have positive results—whether in your professional life or your home life.

**Unleash Your Creativity:
Secrets of Creative Genius**
Rob Bevan and Tim Wright
Infinite Ideas Limited, 2004
256pp ISBN 1904902170

In *Unleash your Creativity*, the authors offer practical ideas to help you to realise your creative potential. In 52 short chapters, it offers advice on building new habits into your professional and personal life that will transform the way you think.

Asking the Right Questions:
A Guide to Critical Thinking: 8th ed.
Neil Browne and Stuart Keeley
FT Prentice Hall, 2006
224pp ISBN 0132203049

This book encourages readers to analyse critically any
information they are given, rather than blindly accepting it. It
suggests different ways of responding to alternative points of
view and will help readers to develop a solid foundation for
making informed choices.

Six Thinking Hats
Edward de Bono
Penguin, 2000
192pp ISBN 0140296662

De Bono represents six different approaches to decision-making
and problem-solving with six 'thinking hats' of different colours:
white (factual); red (emotional); yellow (positive); black (critical
and negative); green (intuitive); and blue (seeing the big picture).
He suggests that by knowing that there are different approaches,
and through role play in which each member of a group literally or
metaphorically wears a different hat, communication can be
improved and the overall effectiveness of the group as a
generator of new ideas can be enhanced.

The Procrastinator's Handbook:
Mastering the Art of Doing It Now
Rita Emmett
Audio Renaissance, 2006
Audio CD ISBN 1593978472

Most people procrastinate to some extent—but it is a
troublesome habit that should be overcome. Using advice drawn
both from her own experiences and those of others, the author
empowers procrastinators to identify the behavioural patterns
they use when putting things off, to apply proven techniques for
achieving goals, and to develop strategies for moving forward.

101 Creative Problem Solving Techniques: The Handbook of New Ideas for Business

James M. Higgins
New Management Publishing, 2006
240pp ISBN 1883629055

This book provides an overview of the most common problem solving tools, to use at the various stages of the problem solving process. The techniques are divided into personal and group techniques, making it easy to find the most suitable approach for the situation.

Cracking Creativity: The Secrets of Creative Genius for Business and Beyond

Michael Michalko
Ten Speed Press, 2001
352pp ISBN 1580083110

In this book the author examines how creative people think, and looks at how to put their secrets to work for you. He has researched hundreds of history's greatest thinkers, from Leonardo da Vinci to Pablo Picasso, and suggests ways of using their techniques in order to become more creative in both our work and personal lives.

The Mind Gym: Wake Your Mind Up

Time Warner Paperbacks, 2005
288pp ISBN 0751536032

An international bestseller, this book helps us to re-examine our mental habits and change them for the better. With hundreds of practical tips and techniques based on applied psychology, it aims to help us to work more efficiently, increase our energy levels, reduce stress, solve problems more easily, influence more effectively, and enjoy life more.

Winning Decisions: Getting It Right the First Time
J. Edward Russo and Paul J.H. Schoemaker
Currency Doubleday, 2001
384pp ISBN 0749922850

This book provides a practical four-step method for making winning decisions. The steps in question are: framing decisions effectively; gathering data that does not simply support existing biases; reaching conclusions based on the data gathered; and learning from experience. *Winning Decisions* also includes questionnaires, 'how to's, worksheets, case studies, and anecdotes to help readers apply the methods straight away.

abilities 4
achievements, celebrating 64
action plans 33
ambiguity 24
analogy, research and 33–4
answers, listening to 25
see also questions
approach, working out the best 29
arguing 26
assumptions 15–16, 25–6
    being aware of 54–5
    being clear about 52
    challenging 34–6
    checking 69–70
    examining 56
attention, focused 39
audiences
    connecting with 71
    understanding 69–70

benefits, assigning monetary values to 52–3
best estimate 52
black hat 13
blue hat 13
bottlenecks, human 4
boundaries, defining 51
brainstorming 30–1, 32, 37
break-even point 49
breaking things down 62–3, 66
briefing people 45–6

cause and effect
    diagrams 5–6
    relationships between 3

celebrating successes 64
chairperson's hat 13
charting causes 4
clarifying questions 23
closed questions 19, 27
coaching conversations 20
communication 71–2
    poor 73
compromise 66
concept fan 5–6
concerns, addressing 74–5
control 65–6
cost/benefit analysis 8, 55, 57
    conducting a 48–57
    pros and cons 49–50
costs 57
    assigning 51–2
    opportunity 53
    see also cost/benefit analysis
creative hat 13

data
    collection of 3
    manipulation of 55–6
data hat 12
different perspectives 11–12
direct costs 51
disaster scenarios 41
diversity
    encouraging 14–15
    value of 16
dynamics, issue 3

efficiency
  cost/benefit analysis
    52
  improving 1
  under pressure 46,
    65
egocentricity 15

facts, sorting out 43–4
factual questions 20–1
failure, fear of 59
fire fighting 1, 3, 8
five whys 6–7
flowcharts 4
four Ps approach 13–14

goals, identifying 61,
  66
green hat 13
gut instinct 43, 55

habits, changing 2, 29
homogenous teams 14
human issues 4

ideas, collecting 31
implementation 4
informative questions
  22
intuitive hat 12
irrelevant facts 43–4,
  46

knock-on effects 10,
  28

language 71–2, 75,
  77
leading questions 22

learning 39
Linton, Ralph 11
listening to others 73–4
logical reasoning 39
long-term effects 53–4

misperception 73
motivation 4

naïve questions 21
net present value (NPV)
  53–4

open questions 20, 27
opportunity costs 53
opposing hat 13
outcomes, agreeing on
  30
over familiarity 11–12
overheads 51

panicking under pressure
  40
paralysis by analysis 9
participation, encouraging
  30
patterns and themes 31
payback period 49
perfectionists 58, 59
performance measurement
  6–7
perspectives
  defining 51
  role play 32
  value of different
    11–12
plans, creating 63–4
political sabotage 60
positive hat 13

power 65–6
present value 53
pressure
    efficiency under 65
    making good decisions
        under 39–47
    short-term 7–8
priorities
    conflicting 60
    sorting out 43
problems
    identifying the source of
        7
    looking at from different
        perspective 10–17
    wrong 8
problem solving
    sticking plaster approach
        4
    using proven techniques
        28–38
    wrong problems 8
procrastination
    avoiding 58–67
    reasons for 59–60
productivity
    end of the day 3
    increasing 1
provocative questions
    22

questions
    addressing 74–5
    asking the right 18–27
    listening to answers
        25
    types of 19–23
quick fixes 1

rate of return 53

recommendations,
    implementing 4
red hat 12
re-evaluation 10
reframing matrix 13–14
relationships, causes and
    effects 3
relevant facts 43–4
research and analogy
    33–4
responsibility, overwhelming
    45
risk analysis 41–2
role-play 32–3, 41
root causes
    analysis of 3–4
    identifying 4
    understanding 2

scores, applying 44
Silent Observer 33
Six Sigma approach 6–7
six thinking hats 12–13
status quo, questioning
    2–3
stereotyping 15–16
sticking plaster approach
    4
successes, celebrating
    64

talking decisions through
    44–5
techniques 12–14,
    39–41
time
    limits 30
    wasting 2
timelines, defining 51
tools 12–14, 39–41

undermining yourself 76

values
  conflicting 60
  monetary 52–3
variable costs 51

waffling 19, 24
weightings, applying 44
white hat 12

yellow hat 13